W9-AUP-737

NOT NECESSARILY THE NEWS

AP/WIDE WORLD

Written by
Al Jean
Billy Kimball
Ian Maxtone-Graham
Elaine Pope
Mike Reiss
Ron Richards
Jeff Zimmer
Carrie Freeman
Rob LaZebnik
David Sacks
Lane Sarasohn
Randall Smoot
and the staff of
"Not Necessarily the News"

NECESSARILY NOT ∧ THE NEWS

Produced by Pat Tourk Lee and John Moffitt

Edited by Billy Kimball

COLLIER BOOKS

Macmillan Publishing Company
New York

Collier Macmillan Publishers
London

Copyright © 1985 by Not the Network Company, Inc.

All rights reserved. No part of this book may be reproduced or transmitted in any form or by any means, electronic or mechanical, including photocopying, recording, or by any information storage and retrieval system, without permission in writing from the Publisher.

Macmillan Publishing Company
866 Third Avenue, New York, N.Y. 10022
Collier Macmillan Canada, Inc.

Library of Congress catalog card number: 85-17400

ISBN 0-02-040710-6

Macmillan books are available at special discounts for bulk purchases for sales promotions, premiums, fund-raising, or educational use. For details, contact:
    Special Sales Director
    Macmillan Publishing Company
    866 Third Avenue
    New York, N.Y. 10022

10 9 8 7 6 5 4 3 2 1

Printed in the United States of America

BOSSU/SYGMA

Original photography by Troy Miller

Photo styling by Bruce Ryan

Photo retouching by Bob Rakita

FOR MICHAEL FUCHS AND IRIS DUGOW

Special thanks to: David Basta at Sygma,
Dick Deneut at Globe Photos,
Holly Jones at AP/Wide World,
Matt Miller at UPI/Bettmann Newsphotos,
and Marcel Saba and Dallas Chang at Liaison,
and everyone else who helped research the photos for this book.

A special thank you to our editor, Barry Lippman.

WORLD LEADERS

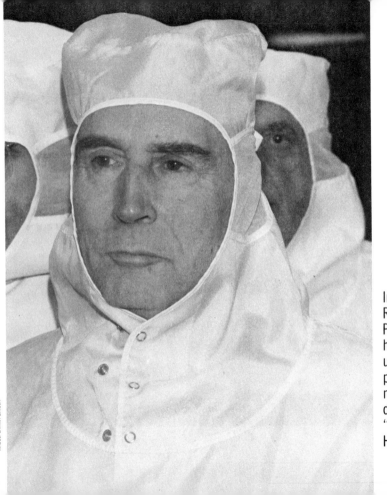

MAQUS GAMMA-LIAISON

Inspired by Ronald Reagan, France's President Mitterand has recently taken up acting. Here he plays an abscessed molar in the traditional Parisian "Pageant of Dental Hygiene."

A miracle occurred in Vatican City last week when a statue came to life and cleaned out the Pope's ears.

GIANSANTI/SYGMA

MATSUMOTO/SYGMA

Thousands of contestants have flocked to Las Vegas for the annual Mother Theresa look-alike contest. Judging categories include healing the sick, feeding the poor, and the veil and swimsuit competitions.

ATLAN/SYGMA

These well-preserved ancient relics were recently put on display in China. Thousands of Chinese are seen here filing past the large dummies in amazement.

Cuban dictator Fidel Castro has abandoned his efforts to quit smoking cigars. "I tried smoking Camels," he explained, "but they smell worse than my cigars, they don't fit in your mouth, and they run away when you try to light them."

SIMONPIETRI/SYGMA

For the fifteenth consecutive year, Niger has been inexplicably passed over for international aid.

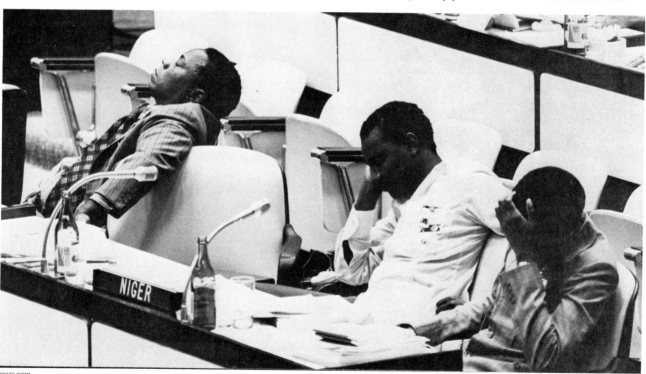

NOGUES/SYGMA

A bout of nerves appears to have overcome Prince Charles, seen here waiting to address visiting dignitaries at Buckingham Palace. "I've gotten used to it," Princess Diana told reporters, "but I do think it sets a bad example for the children."

Some impressive new weaponry was on display around the world this week. The Egyptian Air Force conducted tests of its experimental Stealth Zeppelin *(right),* and the Soviet Army paraded the world's fastest trucks in Red Square *(below).*

MERMET/GAMMA-LIAISON

LAFFONT/SYGMA

Soviet leader Mikhail Gorbachev smiles for photographers.

FRANKLIN/SYGMA

Pope John Paul II examines the world's largest Milk Dud *(left)* and, later, approves a change of habit for the Vatican's nuns *(right)*.

GAMMA-LIAISON

REUTERS/BETTMANN NEWSPHOTOS

Former Greek strong-man Zeus is forcibly removed from office.

Polish union leader Lech Walesa has been stripped of his Nobel Peace Prize after this revealing photo was published simultaneously in *Penthouse* and *Field and Stream*.

KAREL SYGMA

- NO ARTIFICIAL COLORS
- NO ARTIFICIAL FLAVORS
- NO CALORIES • NO CAFFEINE
AND • NO COLA

THE UN-EVERYTHING COLA

New COLA FREE COLA

FOR PEOPLE WHO DON'T WANT—OR NEED— COLA IN THEIR COLA

Even with a worst case Scenario, you look good.

Good (Our Worst)
- Imitation high-impact plastic
- Holds up to 3 lbs. of candy
- Looks just like the real ones

Better
- Hidden compartments
- *Very* expensive leather
- Calculator included
  (no percent key)

Best
- Has it all
- No need to think
- Carries itself

Scenario Luggage
Because living
is the best revenge

PHOTO CREDIT: BRUCE HOERTEL/NEWSWEEK

AP/WIDE WORLD

POLITICS

In an effort to broaden his political base, Mayor Ed Koch welcomes the Hong Kong flu virus to New York.

A large crowd turned out for the final appearance of the George Bush figure at the Washington Wax Museum. The following day it was melted down to make a Cyndi Lauper.

UPI/BETTMANN NEWSPHOTOS

AP/WIDE WORLD

First Lady Nancy Reagan expresses her thanks to Mr. T for his help with her antidrug campaign. Mrs. Reagan told reporters that Mr. T was "her favorite Negro."

House Speaker Tip O'Neill reacts to the prices at the Pentagon Commissary Happy Hour. His Scotch and water cost him $6000.

Controversial ex-Budget Director David Stockman endures his last humiliating punishment administered by the President.

The FBI never rests. A full ten years after his disappearance, they still continue their relentless search for Jimmy Hoffa.

GIANSANTI/SYGMA

MARKEL/GAMMA-LIAISON

UPI/BETTMANN NEWSPHOTOS

THAT'S ABOUT THI

AP/WIDE WORLD

FRANKLIN/SYGMA

UPI/BETTMANN NEWS

IZE OF IT

HAWKINS/SYGMA

AP/WIDE WORLD

Sheraton Centre
New York

UPI/BETTMANN NEWSPHOTOS

MATSUMOTO/SYGMA

AP/WIDE WORLD

President Reagan and
civil rights leader Jesse
Jackson express differing
views as to where the
country is headed.

In this Chinese version of *Hansel and Gretel*, the Wicked Witch pours the children tea before attempting to stir-fry them in a wok.

Vice President Bush's recent visit to Detroit was full of surprises. First, pranksters moved a Port-a-John he had planned to visit during an early morning jog *(left)*, and then his mother turned up at a Republican rally *(below)*. "I thought she was dead," the Vice President commented to reporters.

AP/WIDE WORLD

LOBEAZE

...a new product to relieve an excruciating new complaint ...*EAR LOBE PAIN.*

Pick up LOBEAZE!

NEW

LOBEAZE
CAPLETS

Relieves ear lobe pain faster!

Micro-Thin Coating
extra pain relief
contains no aspirin

PACKAGE NOT CHILD-RESISTANT

50 Caplets·500 mg each

From the makers of NECK AIDS, for the relief of common neck itch, and FOLLICLEX, to soothe those tired hair follicles.

EXTRA-STRENGTH

Fast Relief For Neck Itch
NECK AIDS
ANALGESIC TABLETS

100 TABLETS

FOLLICLEX
OINTMENT

NET WT 2 OZ. (57g)

Prior to their match, tennis ace John McEnroe shakes hands with Pepe, the tennis-playing flea. Later, during a dispute over a line call, Pepe was squashed beneath McEnroe's Nikes.

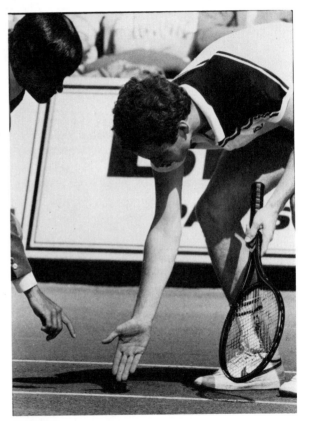

SOLA/GAMMA-LIAISON

Barbra Streisand models costumes from her upcoming film, *Barbrarella II.*

SCHAPIRO GAMMA-LIAISON

The tenth effort by The Mexican Space Administration (TMSA) to land a vehicle on the moon (TLAVOTM) ended in yet another failure when the landing impact killed all 23 astronauts on board.

Members of a bizarre cult of Gumby worshipers gather for evening prayers at their headquarters in the tiny Oregon town of Antelope.

MARK SENNET/PEOPLE WEEKLY © 1985 TIME INC.

"Will the passengers who requested the special meal please identify yourselves to the stewardess."

NACKSTRAND/GAMMA-LIAISON

Overzealous efforts by Alaskan oil companies drilling for new reserves have given Australian farmhand Kevin Beaker an unexpected lift.

REX RDR PRODUCTIONS

Marine Sergeant William "Willie" Foster stands amid the wreckage of his home, which he destroyed in less than 45 minutes. "I lost my keys," explained Foster, "I hate that."

The Defense Department is under fire once again—this time for staff cars customized for the military's top brass. The cars feature a TV, bar, wading pool, dance floor, and bidet and are driven by nonregulation service personnel.

CONRAD/GAMMA-LIAISON

Iowa millionaire farmer and part-time inventor Herb Dunbar has patented a baby-shaped salt lick, which he claims increases licking by 75 percent. "The cows love it, and it looks kind of nice," said Dunbar, who has invested his entire fortune in manufacturing the devices.

Iowa ex-millionaire farmer and part-time inventor Herb Dunbar has come up with a cheap way to manufacture evaporated milk: evaporated cows. "They don't seem to be producing much milk yet," Dunbar confessed, "but, on the plus side, they aren't eating much either."

UPI/BETTMANN NEWSPHOTOS

FRANKEN/S

Iowa ex-dairyman and part-time inventor Herb Dunbar has pleaded innocent to charges of using steroids to fatten up his animals. "I would never do anything strange to an animal," said Dunbar.

The poultry farm at the Iowa State Penitentiary has been the focus of an investigation by the ASPCA. The inmate in charge of the ranch, ex-farmer and part-time inventor Herb Dunbar, was unavailable for comment.

KORODY/SYGMA

ATLAN/SYGMA

Upset by criticism that the network is too liberal, CBS has begun trying to balance their coverage by hiring cameramen from the Ku Klux Klan.

The first (and probably last) Old-Timer's Day at the Indianapolis 500 ended prematurely when 97-year-old driver Swifty "Speedy" Ferguson fell asleep going into the first turn.

Disproving recent rumors that his career is on the skids, charismatic actor Marlon Brando is seen here appearing in *Hamlet Goes Hawaiian* at the Honolulu Dinner Theater.

ONE OF TELEVISION'S BIGGER EVENTS

NIGHT OF ★ 3 OR 4 ★ STARS

WITH
- ★ **LAUREN TEWES***
- ★ **HERVE VILLECHAIZE***
- ★ **PINKY LEE***
- ★ **WINK MARTINDALE***

(*Scheduled to appear)
(May be pre-empted by "Bowling for Dollars" in some areas)

TRY NOT TO MISS IT!
abc
Saturday 9PM on

CREDITS: PETER BORSARI (Tewes) PETER BORSARI (Villechaize) AP/WIDE WORLD (Lee) AP/WIDE WORLD (Martindale)

- ★ You've bought records by Yoko Ono.
- ★ You've bought records by Sean Ono Lennon.
- ★ You've bought records by Julian Lennon.

Now, buy the records of...
JOHN LENNON'S
═ DOG ═

Hear a dog who was
close to the late John Lennon
sing *your* favorite tunes.

DRIVE MY CAR JOHN LENNON'S DOG	NORWEGIAN WOOD JOHN LENNON'S DOG
STRAWBERRY FIELDS FOREVER JOHN LENNON'S DOG	HEY, BULLDOG! JOHN LENNON'S DOG

NORWEGIAN WOOD

JOHN LENNON'S DOG

DRIVE MY CA

HEY **BULLDOG!**
The First Album by John Lennon's Dog

Strawberry Fie
Forever

Buy it today! *The Music of* JOHN LENNON'S DOG

THE PRESIDENT'S WEEK

AP WIDE WORLD

EVANS/SYGMA

9:30 AM
Finding the missing
dry-cleaning ticket for
his pants

1:00 PM
Lunching with South
African black leaders
who later changed
their views on
segregated cafeterias

4:00 PM
Appearing on a
new radio show,
"Who Am I?"

EVANS/SYGMA

KENNERLY/GAMMA-LIAISON

MONDAY

TUESDAY

FICARA/NEWSWEEK

10:00 AM
At a photo opportunity with a life-sized "Knucklehead Smith" doll, a valued possession since childhood

WASHINGTON POST/SYGMA

EVANS/SYGMA

12:00 Noon
Nancy Reagan shows skeptical reporters the giant white rabbits that she claims inhabit the White House.

3:15 PM
All prepared for a cabinet meeting nap

WEDNESDAY

1:30 PM E.S.T.
President Reagan is passed over once again for the Academy Award for "Lifetime Achievement" despite a film career that includes such memorable roles as:

Popeye's grandfather

The mad killer Pruneface in *The Texas Chainsaw Massacre*

And the Talmudic scholar in the all-gentile remake of *The Jazz Singer*

EVANS/SYGMA

AP/WIDE WORLD

KORODY/SYGMA

THURSDAY

AP/WIDE WORLD

11:45 AM
Taking a forceful stand with some demonstrators in front of the White House

3:10 PM
Another busy day at the office

MATHEISON/GAMMA-LIAISON

FRANKEN/SYGMA

10:00 AM
Replanting the cherry tree chopped down by that "reckless ax-wielding liberal" George Washington

1:15 PM
Touring the Reagan museum

EVANS/SYGMA

4:40 PM
Examining the nation's first nuclear hamster

ATLAN/SYGMA

FRIDAY

AP/WIDE WORLD

10:45 AM
Attempting to place a cap on farm price supports

MESAROS/GLOBE

2:30 PM
President Reagan *(left)* saddles
up for a ride around the ranch.

SYGMA

SATURDAY

5:00 PM
Fleeing from the ocean after the President's hair pomade
causes a small oil slick

The First Lady arranges a surprise for the President on his birthday.

AP WIDE WORLD

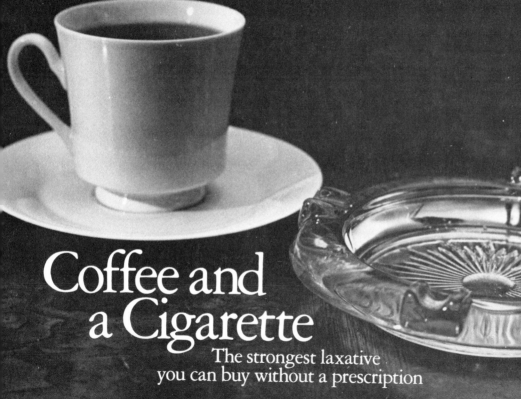

Coffee and a Cigarette

The strongest laxative
you can buy without a prescription

A message from the Coffee and Cigarette Association

MAKE YOUR OWN FUNNY PHOTO

Cut out the pictures you like, combine them in an amusing way, and send the finished product to us. Or, if you prefer, find your own picture, write a caption for it, and send that in instead.

BREESE/GAMMA-LIAISON

KORODY/SYGMA

FRANKLIN/SYGMA

If we use your picture in our next book you will receive a free "Not Necessarily the News" T-shirt, so be sure to specify your shirt size.

Send your picture to:
NOT NECESSARILY THE NEWS
P.O. Box 1469
Los Angeles, CA 90078

AP/WIDE WORLD

AP/WIDE WORLD

Learn How To Do EVERYTHING In The World
...AND MORE!

3.49

The New Best Seller!

THE ULTIMATE SELF-HELP BOOK

(spine) THE ULTIMATE SELF-HELP BOOK

CASLON
PAGEMATIC

PRINTED IN U.S.A.

Now there is a book that tells you how to relax ■ party ■ avoid stress ■ welcome stress ■ diet ■ not diet ■ sleep alone ■ sleep with men ■ women ■ inanimate objects ■ speak French ■ Spanish ■ Pig Latin ■ avoid aging ■ grow up ■ learn self-confidence ■ self-hypnosis ■ self-awareness ■ self-depreciation ■ selfishness ■ how to go to the bathroom ■ spit ■ breathe ■ blow your nose ■ sneeze ■ guess your future ■ guess your weight ■ cook Chinese ■ plant a garden ■ and much, much more.

IT'S THE ULTIMATE SELF-HELP BOOK.

AVAILABLE SOON!